MW00464787

CLAIM
YOUR
SELF

Everyone tells us to communicate better, but no one tells us how
I'm going to tell you how

CLAIM YOUR SELF

MARY WADDELL SUTHERLAND

THE BOX BOOKS

425 Boardman Avenue ▪ Traverse City, MI 49684

Claim Your Self
Mary Waddell Sutherland

©1983 by Mary Waddell Sutherland
All rights reserved

ISBN-13: 978-1475180947
ISBN-10: 1475180942

5 6 7 8 9 10

Cover and interior design by Sandra Salamony

425 Boardman Avenue
Traverse City, MI 49684
231.933.3699
mfsutherland@yahoo.com

Table of Contents

Introduction

Claim Your Self was first published in 1983. At the time, I was teaching at Northwestern Michigan College, conducting workshops, and giving speeches around the state on assertiveness, effective communication, and confidence-enhancing skills for women. This was a second career for me after teaching at the high school level in the Detroit area and then at Glen Lake Community Schools in northern Michigan's Leelanau County. In 1974, I returned to Michigan State (with four children at home, mind you) to earn a master's degree in communication arts and women's studies, with high hopes for solving all the communication problems in the state.

The seventies were an exciting time in northern Michigan. I helped both Connie Binsfeld (former Lt. Governor of Michigan) and Betty Weaver (former Chief Justice of the Michigan Supreme Court) launch their political careers, and had a hand in opening the Women's Resource Center in Traverse City, Michigan. A couple friends and I even started a chapter of the National Organization for Women to the consternation of more than a few men in the region. But most of the excitement was due to the national uproar over equal rights for women. The Pill (contraception), abortion, reproductive rights, violence against women legislation, rape laws, pay equity, paid maternity leave, child support enforcement, breast cancer research, and a pervasive sense in American culture that women were the second sex were the prominent issues of the day.

And still are, unfortunately. Yes, we've made real progress over the past forty years but the gains seem tenuous. Every national election feels like a referendum on battles I thought we won decades ago.

I'm long retired now, happily laying low in Glen Arbor, MI, with grandchildren nearby and a golden retriever named Rosalyn who walks me every day. This new edition of *Claim Your Self* was kick started by my daughter-in-law Victoria, a naturally assertive magazine publisher married to my son Matt. Victoria thought the book might help some women friends who were struggling in their marriages.

Who am I to argue? I hope she's right.

Five Failures
to Communicate

Meet five people who did not successfully control their environment. The unfortunate consequences range from the heartbreaking to the bizarre. One of these individuals could be you. They were all nice people, just trying to get along.

. . . .

Tom was noted for his charm and persuasive personality. He worked as a representative for a large manufacturer in Michigan. Tom, like the rest of us, wanted to make his mark on the world. He did. The headlines in the Detroit papers read: Son Finds Bodies. Couple's Death Called Murder-Suicide.

After 20 years of marriage, Tom's wife, Alice, had recently completed college and started working. With a new career and new friends, Alice decided she wanted a divorce. She was happier than ever and hoping to get more out of life.

One rainy Friday night, Tom came home from work and put two bullets through Alice's head and one through his own. Endless discussions were held among those who knew Tom and Alice. Why? Why had he done it?

• • • • • • •

The second story is about Judy, whose divorce recently became final. A receptionist in a doctor's office, she felt it extremely important to be thought of as sweet. One day an older, very dignified man named Robert came in for his appointment. While he and Judy were talking, he teasingly snapped her bra strap. This annoyed Judy but she didn't say anything. She didn't want to make a scene, after all, he was a respected, prominent man in the community. A week later, Robert came in for another appointment. This time, he cornered Judy and told some very off-color jokes. She did not think they were funny, but she smiled, not wanting to hurt his feelings. Now it just so happened, Robert had a brother, also a distinguished member of the community, who lived at the end of Judy's street. Shortly thereafter, the brother called to say his wife was out of town. He was lonesome. Would Judy like to come down and have a cup of coffee with him, neighborly like?

Judy did not want to go, but she told him she would think about it. Two days later he called again. "I was hoping you would visit. I've got a fresh pot of coffee on the stove."

"Alright," said Judy, "but I can only stay a few minutes."

They had coffee at the kitchen table and a few minutes later he asked her to follow him because he had something to show her in another part of the house. He led her into the bedroom, grabbed her, and attempted to kiss her.

She screamed and ran out of the house. "I'll never go there again," Judy said to a friend, "or let my kids play at that end of the street. I'm always getting myself into these kinds of situations. I just don't understand. Why did he make a pass at me?"

. . . .

The third story is from my childhood. It is about Mrs. Perkins, a woman in her late sixties who was on trial for murder. Mrs. Perkins was a timid, self-effacing, motherly sort of person. Every time I looked at her sitting at the defense table, tears filled my eyes. When court adjourned the first day of the trial, I marched straight to the prosecuting attorney's office. "How can you be so cruel? So heartless? If that dear little woman killed her husband, I'll bet she had a good reason!"

"Yep," answered my father, the prosecutor. "Elmer Perkins was a mean old codger, tended to be physically abusive. In fact, he beat her up pretty regularly, about every Saturday night."

"Why didn't you tell the grand jury not to indict her? That she shot him in self-defense?"

"Hold on there Mary and look at the facts. That dear little woman climbed out of bed on the night of June 9th, loaded the shotgun, and shot her sleeping husband in the head. No matter what sort of no good scoundrel he was, she didn't need to do that."

. . . .

The next story is about Bill, age 29, who told me he was honest with everyone except Barb, the woman he loved and planned to marry. They had been living together for a year. "Barb has many irritating habits," he revealed, "like hanging her hose in the bathroom for days at a time. When they're dry, why can't she take them down at once and put them away? She also likes to stay up late and read, then forgets to turn down the thermostat. But what really bugs me is that she expects me to take care of her car. She was furious the other night, blamed me because she ran out of coolant and the car overheated."

"Have you talked to her about these things?" I asked.

"Absolutely not. I'm afraid if I do, she might move out and not love me anymore."

A year later, Barb came home late one night and found her belongings stacked haphazardly on the front porch. The doors were locked. Bill had kicked her out, decided he didn't want to live with her any longer. The marriage was off. Barb was brokenhearted and to this day does not know why he threw her out.

· · · · · · ·

A friend told me this last story, about the family who lived next door when she was young. Seems the wife nagged and bitched at her husband continually. He was a soft-spoken, long-suffering kind of guy, never said a harsh word back or protested his wife's insufferable behavior. At breakfast one morning, she threw a bowl of oatmeal in his face. Without a word, the man got up and left the room. In a few minutes, he returned and, in front of their four small children, shot his wife in the face.

· · · · · · ·

So what's the pattern of behavior all of these stories have in common?

Would Tom's murder of his wife and his own suicide have happened if, at some point along the way, Tom had expressed his very normal feelings of anger and frustration? What if Alice had gotten more out of life earlier instead of denying her own needs and wasting her potential for twenty years?

When old Robert snapped Judy's bra, did she say, "Cut it out. Keep your hands off my body!"? Nope. And when he told her dirty jokes, did she say, "I don't want to hear them."? Nope. Obviously Robert told his brother about Judy and he took it from there. Her behavior led them to believe she would be open to a come-on. Judy worried more about Robert's feelings than her own. She didn't want to hurt or embarrass him. What about her hurt and embarrassment?

Would Mrs. Perkins, after forty years of marriage, have killed her husband if she had stood up to him the first time he beat her up? What if she had told the parish priest? Her brothers? Called the prosecutor? She did nothing to stand up for herself.

And Mr. Perkins? The old guy might be alive today if he had whipped the tractor instead of his wife.

I believe Bill and Barbara would be married now if Bill had told Barbara about her irritating habits and given her a chance to change.

One wonders why the gentle neighbor man in the last story didn't make it clear on his honeymoon (or before) that he wouldn't tolerate a wife who humiliated or degraded him.

What if she had known how to express her grievances appropriately? Four youngsters were raised in foster homes because the parents never learned to communicate effectively.

Personal damage and regression, as well as personal healing, come through our relationships with others. Whether interpersonal relationships are healthy or dysfunctional is based on communication behavior.

These five individuals made a mess of their lives because they lacked one essential trait for effective communication.

Self-Esteem
and How to Get It

Before I talk about the one essential tool for essential communication, I want to give you an accurate picture of unsuccessful communicators: They are bullies, manipulators, liars, martyrs, or doormats. They feel inferior, lack confidence in themselves, and blame others for their inadequacies.

Successful communicators have self-esteem. They treat themselves with love and respect, which leads them to treat others in loving and respectful ways.

Have you noticed how difficult it is to communicate with individuals who don't like themselves? People with low self-esteem are so absorbed in their own feelings of inferiority and inadequacy, they let others walk all over them or they speak up inappropriately, defensively, or with a chip on their shoulders.

If you think you're not worth much, the tendency is to believe that your feelings, needs, and wants are less important than others. Repressed feelings do not go away. They surface later in one form or another. When you deny, distort, or repress your needs and feelings, your inner sense of integrity is violated.

So self-esteem is the key characteristic of successful communicators. That is all very well. The question is: how do you get some? Not surprisingly, you increase the self-esteem you already have by displaying a sense of self-respect and self-love to the world.

Your self-esteem is increased when you stand up for what you feel is right.

It is important to protest when you are taken advantage of, right? It is appropriate to return a defective item and get your money back, right? It is good to be honest with yourself and others, right? Standing up to someone who is unethical or manipulating the truth is also appropriate, right? To say no when one more obligation will increase your stress or over-extend you is also in your best interests. When you do not stand up for what you feel is right, your self-esteem suffers a blow.

How do you feel about yourself when you have something to say but don't? Do you think, oh well, it doesn't matter? Once, at a public meeting, I said, "I think we'll be opening a can of worms if we commit ourselves to the proposal being discussed." No one paid any attention to me, and the proposal was approved. So be it. I believed I had something to contribute. I did not feel the shame of not speaking up. I acted in a self-respecting manner, shared my opinion. Standing up for what I believed increased my self-esteem.

Self-esteem is increased when you confront someone who is taking advantage of you or someone else.

Saying "no, I won't lend you $20" to the friend who never pays you back is acting in a self-respecting way.

Telling the friend who calls and invites himself for the weekend that it is not convenient increases your self-esteem. This, of course, is the empty-handed "friend" who eats you out of house and home, uses a dozen towels, and arrives with never so much as a piece of cheese or bottle of wine.

Loss of self-esteem and feelings of inferiority happen when you are disappointed or ashamed of your own behavior, not when you disappoint someone else. Self-esteem is your reputation with yourself. When you do not protest or confront someone who is taking advantage of you, you are telling yourself, as well as those around you, who you are. You may feel your behavior doesn't reflect the real you, but what else do you or anyone else have to go on than the actual behavior you display?

My son Matt provided me a painful reminder of how true this is. We had been visiting my mother in southern Ohio, a 12-hour drive, and we were almost home. We passed a bar on the outskirts of a small town and observed a young man and woman scuffling. Matt looked back and said, "Mom, he hit her! Knocked her in the ditch!"

I slowed down. "Oh Matt, let's get on home. She can take care of herself."

"But Mom, you always talk about how we should stand up

for what is right. It's wrong for that man to hit that woman."
The look on his face and his tone said it all.

I swung the car around at the next crossroad and when we returned the young couple was arm in arm and heading back into the bar. If I hadn't gone back, what would my son have learned about his mother? And how would I have felt about myself?

I claimed the real me when we went back.

Emerson said it well: "What you are stands over you the while and thunders so I cannot hear what you say to the contrary."

Each time you are assertive
you gain self-esteem.

I taught an assertiveness training course for many years and several of my students told me their coworkers were upset to hear they had enrolled. "You're already so aggressive I can't stand it! What will you be like when you are through with that class?"

Women reported that their husbands growled, "I didn't know you were so unhappy. I didn't realize you were thinking of a divorce." The women were astounded. They simply thought a course which built confidence and helped them communicate more effectively would enrich their marriages.

As his wife left for the first class, one husband mumbled, "Well, I see you're going to that sandpaper class after all."

"Sandpaper?" asked his wife.

"Yes, where you'll learn to be abrasive."

Assertion is not abrasive, a new game, or a sure-fire way to win an argument. There is no contradiction between politeness, good manners, and assertion. Appropriateness is the key word. Assertion is practiced by people who like themselves enough to claim themselves.

Claiming yourself means honesty in expressing your feelings.

I am hurt.

I am angry.

I am disappointed.

I am irritated.

I am lonely.

I am offended.

I am furious.

I feel very sad today.

I like you.

I love you.

I care for you.

I admire you.

I am attracted to you.

I feel happy.

I am getting mad!

Claiming yourself
means honesty in expressing your needs and wants.

I need time to myself.
I need a pat on the back.
I need some cash.
I need help.
I can hear you. Don't talk so loud.
I want you to stop.
I want a hug.
I want a puppy.
I want to be left alone.
I want to change jobs.

Claiming yourself
means expressing your opinions.

I disagree. This is how I see it...
I am concerned about global warming.
I believe vegetarian diets are healthy.
I am for nuclear power.

You don't have to be a walking encyclopedia to have an opinion. No proof is necessary. It's an opinion, after all. Nor do you need to explain, justify, or defend an opinion, feeling, need, or want. You say what you think and grant others the same privilege. If you have to be right, you will not successfully control your environment. The self-claimer is tolerant of opinions. Arguing or trying to change another's beliefs does not increase your self-esteem. Being right is not worth alienating a friend, colleague, or spouse. Stating and explaining your beliefs or opinions is fine.

Note the use of "I" in the above examples. "I" takes responsibility for what you feel; it does not accuse or blame others. When the word "you" is used, there is going to be a problem.

The problem is communication breakdown.

You hurt me.
You disappoint me.
You make me angry.
You are never on time.
You knew that would upset me.
You drive me crazy.
You make me sick.
You are stupid.
You want to confuse me.
You offend me.

The word "you" is an attack word, and people will defend themselves against attack. "What the heck do you mean I hurt you? I disappoint you? I make you sick? Well, let me tell you, you're not so damn perfect yourself!"

Claiming yourself means you don't ever blame, accuse, or put down your friends or family.

Illustrations

"Mike, you didn't clean your room or make your bed. You live like a pig."

A better way: "Mike, I want you to clean your room. I want your bed made and the trash taken out. I want it done now."

What is the issue? What do you want done? Putting someone down to get what you want usually backfires. No one likes to be attacked, and when it happens, the first instinct is to lash back at the attacker. The "I" message enables Mike to save face and, at the same time, redirect or change his behavior.

"I wish you would kiss me when you come home from work. I think about you all day and can't wait for you to get here."

Not recommended: "You never kiss me or pay attention to me. If I'd known how unaffectionate you are, I would never have married you. You only want me for one thing."

Now do you want a kiss or not? Which message will get you one? There are no guarantees either way but the "I" message is much more likely to get you what you want. Next time your spouse may *feel* like kissing you.

The use of "you" puts the other person on the defensive. "I" allows them to comply without feeling attacked or losing face.

Another important skill in claiming yourself is eye contact. It is rude not to look at the person you're talking to. When people don't look at us, we begin to feel unsure, insecure, and uncomfortable. In fact, some people don't look at us because they want to make us insecure. All the better for them to control us. In the future don't be hesitant to say, "I would like you to look at me."

Eye contact is necessary for another reason. Research shows 60 to 85 percent of interpersonal communication is conveyed nonverbally through expressions on the face, the eyes, body position, tone of voice, gestures, rate of speaking, and inflection, all of which carry more meaning than words. The words may amount to as little as 15 percent. If I don't look at you, I may miss the majority of your message. How then can I respond intelligently?

It is hard to take seriously someone who does not look at us. A woman commented to me once, "I used to go in the living room, look out the window, and tell each member of the family what I wanted them to do. Nobody paid attention. Now I go in, look each one in the eye, say, 'Joe, I want you to peel the potatoes. Timmy, I want you to set the table.' It's like a miracle! They all do exactly what I ask."

Claiming yourself
means you don't send out double messages.

Make sure your words are consistent with your facial expressions, body movements, and tone of voice. When you say something serious, look and act serious. A smirk on your face doesn't fit with, "Hey, I really like your new suit." Smiling or giggling when you're angry is an inconsistent message. How can I take you seriously? When the verbal and nonverbal messages are in conflict, the nonverbal message is believed.

A professional woman told me she flew to Chicago for an

important business meeting. "The men at the meeting did not take me seriously, and I was assertive...do you suppose it was what I wore?"

"What did you wear?" I asked.

"Well, I have this soft, angora sweater with an alphabet block on the front."

Professionals wear business clothes to business meetings. A soft, pink sweater with ABCs across her breast was not appropriate. Unsure in her new role as a businesswoman, she wanted to be sure they realized she was feminine. Seeking to prove your femininity or masculinity is a sure way to sabotage yourself.

People with self-esteem
do not play games.

There is no need to manipulate or intimidate others to get what you want. Think about the people in your life whose friendship you value. Are these friends straightforward and do they say what they mean, or are you confused or vaguely anxious after speaking with them? I wonder what Bill was getting at when he mentioned the boss was running an ad for a new position? Or, was Martha trying to tell me something when she said she's seen my kid hanging around the gas station a lot lately? If she had something to say, why didn't she just say it?

One woman exclaimed, "I've expended so much energy trying to get my husband to say or do what I want him to do. At the same time I try to make him think it's his idea!"

We've all done this. It not only takes energy, but it also makes us feel devious.

Playing games, sending out double messages or "you" messages decreases your self-esteem.

Your self-esteem is increased when:

You stand up for what you feel is right.

You confront someone who is taking advantage of you or anyone else.

You are honest in expressing feelings, needs, and opinions.

You send "I" messages and maintain eye contact.

Your verbal and nonverbal messages are consistent.

Chapter 3

Do Not Reward or Reinforce Bully Behavior

Claiming yourself means not rewarding or reinforcing inappropriate behavior.

The father of one of my students was a doctor. His favorite pie was coconut cream, but sometimes he would come home from the office or hospital and a coconut cream pie would be cooling on the counter and he'd get angry. "For God's sake, another coconut cream pie! I'm sick to death of coconut cream pie. Why the hell don't you make an apple pie once in a while?" He'd rant and rave, stomp around the house, then read the newspaper until dinner. When the pie was served he would murmur, "This is delicious. Thank you for making it. It's my favorite, you know."

"I was little," said Jane, "and I remember telling my mother I didn't understand."

Her mother replied, "Oh, don't you know? When Daddy doesn't like coconut cream pie, it means he lost a patient."

By remaining silent, not protesting her husband's rude behavior, Jane's mother was approving the behavior. Not speaking up reinforced his behavior and, at the same time, enabled her husband to justify it. Since she never protested, he continued the inappropriate behavior. What were the children in that home learning? That it's okay to take out your hurt and frustration on others?

People with a healthy amount of self-esteem do not take out their hurt, anger, disappointment, or sadness on others. If a person in your life does, speak up. If they persist in using you as a whipping post, ignore or detach yourself from the situation. That is, do not allow the person with the problem to give you a problem. You did nothing wrong. Giving them the power to upset you is not claiming yourself. Playing doormat hurts you and the other person.

No one can hurt you, make you angry, or frustrate you unless you allow it. Don't give anyone that power. Behavior is learned and can be unlearned. Try responding in a different way. Take a risk and practice behavior that showcases who you really are.

An elderly man came to see me for advice. "Every time a new committee is formed or there is a vacancy on a board in my county, I'm asked to serve. I always say yes and I'm worn out!" He was the type of guy who always got the job done and never said no, so naturally he was asked often. The point is, you have the right to refuse requests. Only you know how hectic your life is.

Fundamental to claiming yourself is looking inside your

head first to get clear on what you want, feel is right, or is in your own best interest. Having determined what you want, look carefully at what others expect from you. You can then evaluate the consequences of your action and decide. Claiming yourself is making a choice.

When you do choose to assert yourself, look the person in the eye and say, "No, I won't run for the school board. Thank you for asking." Do not give reasons or try to justify your decision. If reasons are given, the other person will only counter them, try to change your mind to get you to do what he wants you to do. If you simply say no, they won't have the ammunition needed to shoot you down.

For example: "Martha, the nominating committee got together and every one of us came up with your name for president! You will run, won't you?"

"That's very flattering, but I've been so busy lately. I don't really have the time to do a good job."

"I knew we could count on you! Even a job half-done from you would be better than what we've had. I can't wait to tell the rest of the committee."

One former PTA president told me she served a year and hated every minute of it. "I tried to say no," she said, "but no one paid any attention."

"What happened?" I asked.

"I didn't want to make a scene. There were a lot of people standing around."

"A few seconds of embarrassment against a whole year of serving in a job you hated?"

"I wish I'd had the guts to be firm," she said. "It was the worst year of my life."

This woman was guilty of thinking terrible things would happen if she stood up for herself. Her belief that the worst would happen prevented her from saying no.

It is extremely important to imagine positive results: *The person asking will graciously accept my no, and that will end it.* What you imagine and believe will invariably come true.

The person asking favors or making requests would prefer you to say yes because, otherwise, he must ask someone else. Pressing your buttons and getting a yes from you makes life much easier for him.

When faced with a bully or manipulator, remain calm and in control. Stick to your guns. Being true to yourself makes you feel proud and increases your self-esteem.

Unclaimed People Are Phonies

A friend shows up forty-five minutes late for lunch and says, "Gosh, I'm sorry. I hope you didn't mind waiting."

"No, I didn't mind. I brought a book to read," you say.

The truth is, you did mind. You looked at your watch a hundred times and worried that you misunderstood the meeting place. As the minutes ticked by, you got progressively more anxious, frustrated, helpless. The self-claimer is honest. "I expected you at noon. It is 12:45. I don't like to be kept waiting." Your intention is not to put the other person down. Simply express how you feel. In doing so, you demonstrate self-respect. The friend can explain, apologize, whatever, and you will listen. It is much easier to accept someone else's behavior when you feel good about your own. Saying nothing, denying your own feelings, is not claiming yourself. When you beat around the bush and avoid the plain truth, you tell yourself and others, "I am not important. Your feelings, needs, opinions take precedence over mine." Behaving this way is phony. It is also self-destructive.

"Men ask me to sleep with them and I don't want to hurt their feelings, so I say yes," said a woman in her twenties. "Most of them have no respect for me and I hate it."

This woman was facing a second abortion. Eventually, she learned to tell the truth about her feelings, and slowly her reputation with herself was rebuilt.

On the way home from work, John thinks about his wife: *I haven't been very attentive lately. Maybe I should ask Betty if she wants to go out to dinner. God, I hope she doesn't want to go.*

He comes in the house. "Honey, would you like to go out to dinner?"

Betty doesn't want to go either. The chicken is half thawed, dessert is made, and she was going to write a letter to her mother. She answers, "Good idea, sweetie. Where shall we go?"

They go out, and all through the meal they argue. By the time they get home, neither one is speaking to the other.

What happened? Both were lying. Both were guilty of doing what they thought the other wanted. Denying your own wants (or lying about them) leads to self-contempt. You blame the other person when in reality you're angry with yourself. This kind of dishonesty causes communication problems in relationships. Over a period of time, it can result in a breakup. Trying to be nice at your own expense causes deep resentment. The nice person (after denying her needs or wants for days, weeks, months) frequently becomes mean and vindictive. Remember the man whose wife threw the bowl of oatmeal in his face? His behavior illustrates the extreme and there are many variations in between. The point is, emotional dishonesty is harmful to all involved.

Get in touch with yourself. Many people are so out of touch with their feelings, needs, and wants that they are unaware of the lies they tell. Or, they express anger or yell when the actual emotion they are feeling is hurt or sadness. A wife crying over the death of a favorite relative may hear her husband exclaim, "Can't you control yourself? Stop that sniffling." He attacks her instead of admitting his own grief at the death of a relative he too loved. He may not even know he is sad and hurting, having denied his real feelings for years. Unclaimed people are afraid they will lose face if they express emotions (other than anger), so they lash out at others instead. They do not realize that eventually family and friends will withdraw from them. Who wants to be around a phony, especially when the phony is mean? Unclaimed people have few close friends. In many cases their spouses tire of their behavior, lose respect for them, and leave.

The opposite of love is not hate, it is apathy. When things turn sour in a relationship, one partner simply does not care any longer. If she has to interact with a husband who lacks self-esteem, she responds superficially and will often comply just to get him off her back.

The phony (who behaves aggressively) talks loud and fast, stands too close, and uses his body and voice to intimidate.

He wants to feel powerful and will do whatever is necessary to get his way or be right. The phony (who behaves non-assertively) usually gives in, but may later get back at the bully in subtle, hidden ways. If they both choose to display aggressive behavior, the situation can end up in a dramatic fight. Aggressive and passive people are insecure. People who feel good about themselves do not behave this way. They do not lie, manipulate, or have anything to prove. All of us display unclaimed behavior at times. When you are committed to claiming yourself you begin to recognize your self-esteem. Most of us display our authentic selves when we are optimistic and feeling good. When we are down or unsure, we tend to let others take advantage of us, or we take advantage of them.

The aggressive-type phony puts being right above maintaining or establishing healthy relationships. Bullying makes them feel good for a short time. Later, the aggressive person may evaluate his behavior and feel ashamed or guilty. Neither of these emotions are a source of pride.

Many years ago my husband and I were invited to a dinner party. All evening one of the guests baited me, tried to put "that assertive woman" in her place. "Admit it, Mary, the husband should be the head of the house. Masculine men let their wives know who is boss."

Every chance he got, he slipped in a remark, trying to get a rise out of me. I saw no sense getting caught up in his game, so I held my tongue. As we were leaving, he followed us to the front door and began again.

"You know I'm right, don't you? Real men rule the home!"

"Harry," I said, "you are a real man, as masculine as you can be. You've got the right physical apparatus, you've got your penis. You don't have to prove a thing."

His face turned purple and he stomped back into the living room. A few days later, I ran into his wife. "Harry has talked about you ever since the dinner party. He thinks you are wonderful." I walked down the street smiling. Of course he does. I called his bluff. I confirmed that he had a penis. He no longer is driven to prove his masculinity.

When we don't behave as some people want us to, they resort to calling us names. Here's the definition for bitch, weird, and crazy: *What someone calls you when you are not behaving as they want you to behave.* Name calling is probably the easiest way to manipulate others. "What must I do to make you stop calling me a bitch?" If you feel you must prove you are not a bitch you give the name caller control over your actions.

Claiming yourself means accepting the primary human right: *I have the right to decide what is appropriate behavior for me.*

Only you know what is right for you, how you feel, and what you like. Early in our marriage, my husband used to say to me, "I know you better than you know yourself. I know you'll hate this movie."

I would nod in agreement but would harbor an almost unconscious resentment. One day, I protested. "Hey! That is very presumptuous of you. You don't know me better than I know myself. Don't ever say that again." He never did.

People who don't stand up for themselves, who let others make decisions for them, lose self-respect and their self-esteem takes a nose dive.

Ernest Becker in *The Denial of Death* writes, "What a person needs most is to feel secure in her self-esteem." Throughout this book I've illustrated how people lose what they need most. Behavior which violates your rights or the rights of others is not presenting the real you. It's phony.

Uncovering Yourself

Crucial to claiming yourself is a commitment to stop hiding from yourself. A lack of self-understanding results in unclear messages to others; it is a guarantee that you will not successfully control your environment. You cannot communicate with others until you first learn to communicate with yourself. What do I want? How do I feel? What are my needs, my opinions, my goals? If you don't know the answer to these questions, how on earth are you going to express the proper emotion?

I recommend keeping a journal and getting to know yourself. By keeping a record, you will find that in certain situations you wear a mask, disguising the real you. Are you self-effacing with your doctor? Dogmatic and intimidating with your children? Do you suddenly become inhibited and awkward with the PhD down the street? Why? Are you under the silly belief that those with advanced degrees are better than the rest of us? My wise father said often, "Some of the dumbest people I have ever met have PhDs and some of the smartest never saw the inside of the eighth grade."

It is extremely important to be aware of your own phoniness. Self-awareness enables you to change, to bring your behavior in line with who you really are.

A businessman stopped me on the street one day: "I want to thank you. I was living with a non-person. My wife didn't have a thought, need, or opinion of her own. I was so bored with her I was going to leave. Now she is behaving like a person. We are happier than we've been in years."

This man's wife was authentic in her other roles. She held a professional job and was on a number of civic committees. Only in her marriage did she display phony, inhibited, and self-denying behavior. Claiming yourself means being yourself no matter who you are dealing with, no matter what the situation.

The stance of the self claimer is: *I am not better than you, nor less than you. We are equal.* After marriage, some women change and begin almost unconsciously to play a subordinate role. Society expects this role-playing, and women are socialized to meet those expectations. But this ridiculous cultural norm backfires. Many divorced women tell me they play-acted the perfect wife role. They submerged and repressed themselves to the point of losing sight of who they once were. The person their husband married disappeared, and he lost interest and threw his wife out in the cold.

One woman's story is particularly tragic. Her husband was a writer. She typed and edited his manuscripts and kept five children out of his way so he could write in peace and quiet. She did all the cooking, cleaning, washing, yard work, even learned to fly (though she was terrified). "I thought I was content," she told me, "to be the woman behind the man. Everything I did was to please him, to make him happy. I compromised myself so much that I lost sight of who I am."

He left her shortly after the sixth child was born, for an older, dynamic, self-actualized woman.

This, of course, works both ways. The man who talks a good story before marriage often does a change of face two weeks after the honeymoon. He dominates, controls, sets limits on his wife's activities, and becomes the macho male. Because she loves him and wants to preserve the marriage, the wife may revert to childlike behavior. Twenty years later, she comes to her senses, reclaims herself, and leaves. She had lost respect for him years earlier. She didn't hate him, she just didn't care. Emotionally, she had begun to detach herself from him while waiting for the children to grow up. When they did, she found a job and decided he was a problem not worth trying to solve any longer. If you want to know why we have a high divorce rate in this country, the above examples explain a great deal. Not being real, playing games, and wearing false faces all cause the breakup of most relationships.

All behavior is learned.

Communication behavior is learned. You've been imitating, trying out, and practicing various methods of communicating since the day you were born. In all likelihood, you have adopted verbal and nonverbal habits which disguise who you really are. The women's rights movement has made tremendous changes in the way men and women communicate with each other. Filing for divorce is communication. Fifty years ago women rarely took this step in revealing their unhappiness and discontent. The stigma against divorced women made even the thought of such a thing too painful. Culturally, men have been allowed to leave their wives since the earliest days of marriage. Today, the wife is as likely to leave as the husband. The difference between men and women is that husbands are left to lick their wounds alone. Women have friends who understand, console, and support.

Men tend to keep each other at a distance and are not emotionally honest with each other. They seldom reveal pain, sadness, and failure to other men. Slowly but surely this is changing. I see it in the men who are willing to take the risk and claim themselves.

"Basically my boss is a kind and decent man," said an executive secretary. "I see that side of him, but with the rest of the staff he's a tyrant, yells a lot, is demanding, seems to enjoy putting people on the spot and making them look bad in front of others. I've heard through the grapevine that his wife is filing for a divorce."

She persuaded him to make an appointment at my office. After a few weeks, his outer behavior did demonstrate the basically "kind and decent" man he was on the inside. It took a while but he claimed himself and no longer feels compelled to play the stereotypical male role in our society. His wife dropped her suit for divorce.

There is great pain and fear in both men and women

today. The old ways no longer work. Men are more resistant to change than women, but change they must. Women cannot do this for them. Claiming yourself is a do-it-yourself process. When you get in touch with your feelings and understand your needs and wants, you will discover yourself.

• • • • •

To be nobody but yourself in a world which is doing its best, night and day, to make you everybody else means to fight the hardest battle which any human being can fight; and never stop fighting.

e. e. cummings

Reclaiming Your Self

You cannot change someone else's behavior, but you can change your reaction to that behavior. Don't let them give you a headache or force you to muddle through life trying to figure out what you are doing wrong. The person who picks at you, puts you down, manipulates, or bullies you has the problem, not you.

The one you love may be tired and overworked. This does not give them the right to make you suffer. Speak up! "I know you are tired or had a bad day, but I feel hurt when you blame me for something I had nothing to do with. I will not be your whipping post." That's all you need to say. You did nothing wrong.

If the other person persists, look them in the eye and say, "Stop yelling at me." Do not argue that you too had a hard day. Doing this only diverts you both from the real issue. It doesn't matter who had the hardest day.

"I'm sorry." "I apologize." "I made a mistake." These phrases are used by people who claim themselves. When you do something wrong, admit it. Do not become defensive.

You know you are human. You do not have to be perfect to feel good about yourself.

Unclaimed people expect perfection in themselves. Claiming yourself means giving up the irrational belief that you must be 100 percent competent 100 percent of the time. Acknowledging imperfection in yourself makes it easier to control your responses to other peoples' behavior and to accept imperfection in them.

Live in the here and now.

If your spouse says, "For God's sake, you forgot to pick up the cleaning! You are so inconsiderate. I can't count on you for anything," try to simply respond with, "Hey, I'm sorry. I'll pick it up tomorrow." Refuse to make excuses or offer a lot of reasons for your behavior. It's already happened. You can't do anything about it.

Controlling your behavior and taking responsibility for your actions frees you from all the whys and maybes going on in your head: *Maybe he doesn't care for me anymore. Why did he do that? What did I do that made him angry?* Dwelling on thoughts like this is not in your best interest.

I arrived home from class one day and the phone was ringing. When I answered, a woman's hysterical voice carried on about how upset she was. "I had to call you. I knew that if I didn't call, I would never come to your class again."

"Why?" I asked. "What happened?"

"You gave me a disapproving look this morning. I've gone over and over everything that happened in class. I simply must know what I did to deserve it."

"Martha," I answered, "the clock is above your head. I probably realized I would not be able to complete my lesson plan and a frown crossed my face in your direction."

"Oh," she said. "I am so relieved."

Good for Martha. She recognized her real feelings and did something tangible to help herself. But why was Martha so vulnerable that a disapproving look would upset her? She was attractive and talented, a member of the Detroit Symphony. She was trapped in the irrational need to be perfect and she also needed to be loved and approved by everyone to feel good about herself. About 99 percent of the population is caught up in this one. Have you ever been at the supermarket and the cashier frowns and looks at you with a question in her eyes and you wonder all the way home if you did something wrong? Have you shopped in a clothing store and been ignored or had a clerk who was cold? I have and it was awful. *What is wrong with me? Aren't I dressed properly? Did I say or do something stupid?* I no longer give incidents like this a second thought.

No matter who you are or what you do, there are going to be people who don't like you. So what! It's okay not to be loved and approved by everyone. The only one whose love and approval you need is your own. You are all you have. If your behavior is acceptable in your eyes, that is what counts. Robert Morley said, "To fall in love with yourself is the first secret of happiness. I did so at 4½ and if things don't go too well, I can always fall back on my own company." Morley is a very wise man.

Claiming yourself
means believing you have rights:

I have the right to love and be myself.
I have the right to be the final judge of what's best for me.
I have the right to do dumb things.
I have the right to be wrong.
I have the right to have fun.
I have the right to change.
I have the right to do anything as long
as it doesn't hurt anyone else.
I have the right to say no.

There are many more. Add your own. If you believe you have those rights, then take a risk, and act on them.

Who is going to be hurt if you say no to taking a friend home from work everyday?

If you resist sexual overtones?

If you say no to the neighbor who constantly borrows your things?

If you agree to take a friend home from work everyday and it robs you of precious time, who is it going to hurt? You! Why do you keep hurting yourself?

When you say yes and mean no, your self-esteem is damaged. Your friends may be hurt and angry, but what about the hurt and anger you will feel if you deny your own feelings and needs? When you do, you state that other people are more important than you. The self-claimer stance is: *My needs, feelings, and wants are on a level with the rest of the world. Sometimes my needs take precedence. It is not mean or selfish to consider my needs. When I deny them, my message to others is that they are better or of more value. This is a lie.*

Don't Let Fear Stop You

It is difficult to tell a friend that she has done something that bothers you because she may become defensive or upset. The need to be loved and approved of is a powerful force. Remember, your intent is to be honest. Speaking up is healthy, is acting in your own best interest. Speak with an "I" message, keep it short, be specific, and bring up only one issue. Do not belabor the point or accuse your friend of hurting you purposely. Here's an "I" message example: "I wish you had called. I was worried. I didn't know where you were."

And not the following: "You didn't call. You knew I would be upset. You never think of me. You caused me to look like a fool because I didn't know where you were. You are always doing this to me."

In this example, two words along with "you" are guaranteed to put the other person on the defensive: "always" and "never." *You never think of me; you always do this to me.*

How do you feel when someone says to you, "You always

forget my birthday." *It just isn't true. At least once, in forty years, I remembered your birthday!*

"You never take me out for dinner." *Ouch! That hurt. I've taken you out before and you know it.*

"Should" is another loaded word. We "should" all over ourselves. Stop using never, always, and should. When you remove these three words from your vocabulary, there will be a noticeable change for the better in your relationship with others.

When someone criticizes you, do not let them have the power to make you mad and lose sight of the real issue.

There are two things to remember when being criticized: 1) look the person in the eye, and 2) shut your mouth.

Shut your mouth and allow the other person to get what's bothering them off their chest. If you interrupt before they have finished, the issue is not resolved, an argument results, and both parties are frustrated. Hear the person out and then determine whether the criticism is valid or not. If it is not, say so. If it is valid, admit it. Again, be brief and low key.

"You were late for dinner three times this week."

"That's right. I was late for dinner three times this week. I'm sorry."

The other person has the right to speak up about what affects him just as you do. Holding back is destructive to both of you. Invariably, the problem surfaces later. It may be disguised, or worse, blurted out with a dozen other held back complaints.

Claiming yourself means letting go of positive feelings as

well as negative ones. It means saying, "I really appreciated your listening to me. I needed a sounding board."

"I enjoyed our lunch together. I am so glad you are my friend."

"I think your new haircut looks wonderful on you."

"I am so pleased you called. I get a lift just hearing your voice."

"I believe you are the most organized person I have ever known. I admire your ability to accomplish so much."

If you are stingy with compliments, or forget to praise others, they will find it extremely difficult to hear your criticism.

A group of people persuaded one of their coworkers to take my assertive training class because Molly, another member of the staff, was driving them all crazy. Molly was a compulsive tapper. She tapped her feet, her pencil, her fingers, and was in noisy motion from eight to five each day. Everyone in that office was suffering side effects (headaches and depression) because of Molly's antics.

"Has anyone talked to Molly?" I asked.

"Heavens no," replied Susan. "Molly is such a nervous wreck she would probably scream and throw her pencil at whoever spoke up. We can't even imagine leveling with her. She might become even worse, although I don't know how that would be possible."

I suggested that Susan simply walk over to Molly's desk and say, "I am bothered by your tapping. I wish you would stop."

Eventually, Susan got up the confidence to confront Molly. Molly was stunned. "What tapping? Do I tap? I didn't realize it."

A lot of us have nervous mannerisms of which we are not aware. If no one tells us, we are not given a chance to correct them. Molly didn't stop her tapping overnight, but within a short time no one in that office went home with a headache because of her tapping.

Susan spoke calmly and was clear and brief in stating the problem. She did not go into detail or explain or defend her reasons for bringing up her complaint. If she had, Molly might have become defensive or felt ashamed. Susan did an excellent job.

What was the issue here? Not headaches or everyone going crazy. The issue was: stop the tapping.

A bank manager at a seminar asked me about one of her tellers. "Every time I look at Polly she's talk, talk, talking or giggling about something. She doesn't get her work done and I may have to fire her."

"Have you talked to her?"

"Oh yes! She got very defensive and upset. It was awful."

"What did you say to her?"

"Well, I said, 'Polly, every time I look at you, you're talking and laughing and I want you to stop it.'"

"No wonder she got upset. Polly's talking and laughing was not the issue."

The bank manager gave me a puzzled look. "It wasn't?"

"No. The issue is Polly not getting her work done. You can

talk to her about that. You expect the deposits to be recorded by three o'clock, the new accounts registered, etc. Talk to her about her job responsibilities. That's the issue."

It is necessary to get a clear handle on the issue before you approach the person. Ask yourself: What is it I want to happen? What do I want to accomplish by talking to this person? What behavior do I want stopped?

The bank manager wanted the teller to get her work done. The talking and laughing were incidental and would probably cease as the teller became more conscious of completing her work.

Jack, a physical therapist, bought his wife a sixty dollar purse for Christmas. She did not like it, so he took it back to the store. The sales clerk smiled and said, "Fine, you can exchange it. We have a no refund policy."

"There is nothing in the store I want," he told the class. "It's not fair."

"Did you tell the sales clerk you wanted your money back?" asked a student.

"Well, no. I just told him my wife didn't like the purse."

"What's the issue? What do you want?" pressed a student.

"My money back! Sixty dollars is a lot of money."

He went back the next day, handed the clerk the receipt, and said firmly, "I would like a refund."

"I'm sorry, we have a store policy," said the clerk, "no refunds, only exchanges." Jack looked around and noticed the purse was gone.

"I see you sold my wife's purse," said Jack. "You got your

money, I want mine."

The clerk immediately went to the cash register and handed him his money.

Was Jack taking advantage of the clerk? No. Even if the purse hadn't been sold, he had the right to his money.

A school bus driver said a little boy borrowed a dime from him one morning weeks ago and had not paid him back. "It's not the money," he said. "I think kids should learn that if they borrow money they must pay it back."

"Did you ask him for it?" I asked.

"A number of times. In a kidding way, I've said, 'Hey Billy, you got my money yet?'"

"Do you want your dime or not?" I asked. "Tomorrow, look Billy in the eyes and say 'I want my dime by Friday.'"

Billy gave him the money the next day.

All of these examples point out the importance of getting clear on the issue. What is it you want? Figure it out and say it. There are no guarantees the other person is going to comply, but a positive outcome is much more likely when a clear message is received.

Self-esteem is increased when people hear you and take you seriously, for you are influencing and controlling your environment. The reward may be as little as a dime or as much as a sane workplace, but either way you are rewarded.

Talking about the things you are afraid to talk about is worth the risk. Your self-esteem soars when others respond in a positive manner. When they don't, you can feel good about the fact that you tried.

There is no such thing as perfect communication. Even the most well-presented message may fall on deaf ears. You can never predict a response. All you can do is strive to make yourself clear.

Actions and Reactions

Claiming yourself is being responsible for controlling both your actions and reactions. Did you know your reactions reveal more about you than your actions? Our actions are often planned or decided beforehand, while our reactions (to another's behavior) are spontaneous. The spontaneous reaction, when inappropriate, is usually blamed on the other: "She made me angry! If she hadn't done that, I wouldn't have thrown her across the room!"

Your four-year-old son talks back and you strike him. His sassy mouth made you do it, right? He's responsible for your uncontrollable reaction, right? Wrong! You are responsible.

Rarely do people who are important to each other level about irksome reactions and grievances. Most of the time we withhold our feelings because we fear making someone angry or being rejected by the other. So they continue the same behavior, unaware of our true feelings, and we continue our same behaviors, oblivious to the effect our actions have on them. Keeping our mouth shut or spewing out some smart, sarcastic remark denies, evades, or covers up what is really transpiring. This pattern is symptomatic of a communication problem that, if not dealt with, will cause a complete relationship breakdown. Caring about the other means you level with them rather than withhold or distort honest responses.

Sending flowers, cooking a favorite meal, taking a child to Disneyland instead of apologizing for your inappropriate reaction only exacerbates the problem. "I don't want the flowers!" "I am choking on my favorite meal!" "Yes, I did want to go to Disneyland but how come I'm not having fun?"

Cowardly attempts to heal snarled communication usually cause the relationship to go downhill fast. An accumulation of little irritations, bruised feelings, misunderstandings, and defensive outbursts end most relationships.

Time does not heal all wounds.

Suggestions for leveling with others:

1 Your intent must be a desire to improve the relationship. If your intent is to prove you're right, show how intelligent you are, or arouse guilt in the other person, the interaction will fail. Convey that the relationship means everything to you and that you want to improve it because it is important. At the same time, make it clear that you want to know how the other person perceives and feels about your actions/reactions.

2 Share your reactions as near to the time of the behavior as possible. Sleeping on it or hoping it will resolve itself in time avoids the issue, enabling resentment to build up. When we postpone, we tend not to bring it up at all. In sharing your reactions, choose the best time for you. That means when you feel serene, rested, and in control of yourself. Too often, we tend to pick the best time for the other person. For example, I would wait until I had everybody fed, the kids bathed and in bed, and the dishes done, before I would talk to Dale. By that time, I was a frazzled wreck.

3 Paraphrase the other's remarks (about your behavior) to make sure you understand them, and encourage the person to do the same. She said: "You don't like my friend Sally? You're upset because I spend so much time on the phone with her?" He said: "No, no, that's not what I'm upset about. What I'm upset about is that you sound so different when you talk to her. You laugh and joke. You're not that way with me."

4 Be specific rather than general when discussing the other's actions. "You bumped the end table and spilled my coffee," rather than, "You never watch where you're going." Be tentative rather than absolute. "You seem ambivalent about..." rather than, "You don't give a damn about..." Inform rather than demand. "I hadn't finished speaking," rather than, "Stop interrupting me!" Express your concerns in neutral, non-judgmental terms. Use "I" statements constantly. "John, you're saying nothing is wrong, but I'm feeling hurt and confused because you didn't speak to me at all during dinner." The word "you" is aggressive when it makes an assumption. It is not aggressive when it states a fact: "You bumped the end of the table and spilled my coffee."

5 Reaffirm your love and affection for the other person during the tense times and separate the action/reaction that's causing you the pain. "Ruth, I love you very much, but when you lie to me I feel frustrated and angry."

Once you are committed to claiming yourself, the message you wish to convey becomes more and more automatic. Claiming yourself is being responsible for your actions as well as your reactions to others in your life.

• • • • •

Our lives are original documents which we alone can create.

Leo Buscaglia

The Benefits to You and Those You Love

A friend who claimed herself announced, "I bought a number of items the other day at 50 percent off and saved a bundle of money. I bought two wedding gifts, a baby gift, and three birthday presents. I was so excited. When I got home, I told my husband about the sale and he went through the roof. I shut up after telling him about one gift and let it go. A few years ago, I would have been worried sick over whether I had done the right thing. Now I know I did the right thing and don't even think about it. My husband will be very pleased when the time comes to wrap and present the gifts."

"You didn't ask permission or get approval before spending the money?"

"Nope," she answered. "I'm an excellent manager of money, not a spendthrift or frivolous, as my husband has always implied. And the funny thing is, I was telling my neighbor about the sale and my husband heard me. He said, 'You shouldn't have done it.' I said, 'Yes I should have and did. I don't want to hear another word about it.' He closed his mouth and an expression I have never seen before passed over his face."

I smiled. "A look of respect?"

"Yep, exactly. I feel like I've grown up." She laughed. "It's about time, isn't it?"

Claiming yourself means behaving as an adult, not a child.

An optometrist claimed himself when, after ten years of being asked to speak at an annual conference, he said yes. He no longer worried about being 100 percent competent 100 percent of the time. He finally had the confidence to do the best he could and he realized he did not have to be perfect. He accepted himself and with that came the self-confidence necessary to do what many people consider is the number one fear of all people: speaking in public.

When I began teaching assertive training, I worried there might be a rash of divorces in the Grand Traverse area. The opposite occurred. Claiming yourself has a healing effect on troubled relationships. Many husbands and wives tell me that an increase in self-esteem brought them closer together. The positive effects are there, even if only one partner makes changes. There is a ripple effect. Spouses and children are influenced to change. People tell me their parents, sisters, brothers, and close friends become more honest and stop playing games.

One couple who divorced remarried. "For the first time we are really communicating," he told me.

I would be lying if I told you claiming yourself protected you from divorce. Divorce can happen when one partner changes and the other refuses to accept or adapt to those changes. We are all constantly growing and changing. Growth is a part of life. The person who says, "I liked you better before," means, *I want you to behave the way I think best.* Letting someone get away with this will cause you to hate them and you.

Strain in a relationship is to be expected when one partner changes, but this is not cause for divorce. Hang in there and do not give up. I find if you can weather the storm for a year or two, the storm becomes a light rain. No relationship is perfect. It is irrational to expect complete happiness. What you want is a palatable relationship. It does not have to be delicious to be good.

A surprising benefit of claiming yourself is that it shows in your face. I have seen both men and women transformed. Strain disappears, eyes sparkle, and inner grace is manifested. In a few cases I've seen voices change. One woman's pitch was so shrill that every time she spoke everyone around her became noticeably uncomfortable. I spoke to her about lowering her pitch and explained how it was done. In the beginning there was little change. As the class progressed, she increasingly began to act in her own best interest. In her case it meant expecting more from her husband and children and less from herself. The shrillness disappeared from her voice. "I can't get over how people are listening to me now," she mused.

There is a strong probability that after claiming yourself you will achieve your goals. Without self-esteem, without believing you are worthy of success, you won't be able to plan your life or set goals. You will tend to coast, letting life happen to you rather than taking charge and making life what you wish it to be. One reclaimed woman became a doctor, another a lawyer, others nurses and medical assistants.

One mother reported that since claiming herself she is much nicer to her children. "When I walked out the door this morning my son said, 'Mama, you aren't so mean to us kids any more.'"

"It's true," she said. "Respecting my own needs and feelings has made me much happier, much nicer."

True communication is talking about the things we are afraid to talk about. Those who claim themselves are no longer afraid. They know that it's what is left unsaid that determines the nature of relationships. If I don't tell you what pleases me in bed, it is what I do not say that determines whether I have a joyous, fulfilling sex life or am frustrated and unsatisfied.

A woman who had been married for thirty years told me the following story. "Every time my husband and I sat down to dinner and began to eat, he would say, 'Is there any more strawberry jam?' I would jump up, run to the refrigerator and get the strawberry jam. I would get seated again and he'd say, 'Are there any more of those pickles Aunt Martha brought over?' I would hop up, pull out a chair so I could reach the top of the cupboard, and get the pickles. He'd eat a pickle or two and say, 'I sure would like a piece of that home-made bread to go with these pickles.' I would get up, hurry to the bread box, and bring a slice back to the table. I never in thirty years ate an uninterrupted meal.

"Last night, he said, 'Is there any more strawberry jam?' I kept my head down, continued to eat and responded, 'It's in the fridge.' And do you know what? He got up and got the strawberry jam! Later, he said, 'Isn't there any more gravy?' I said, 'It's on the stove.' And do you know what? He got up, went to the stove, and filled the gravy bowl!"

It was what was unsaid that spoiled her dinner hour for thirty years. He was not a son-of-a-bitch. He obviously did not mind getting up for himself, but as long as he had a gopher, he was content to let her serve him.

Claiming yourself means laughter and fun in your life. Do it.

About the Author

Best known for her public speaking, Mary Sutherland has given hundreds of speeches, workshops, and seminars on assertive communication to hospitals, banks, schools, real estate agencies, and other businesses across Michigan.

She was also an instructor in the extended education department at Northwestern Michigan College, for Elder Hostel groups, and for the Leelanau Center for Education.

Mary is the mother of five sons and one daughter. Her husband, Dale, died in 1980 of adrenal cancer. Active in women's issues all her life, she is one of the founding members of Traverse City's Women's Resource Center. In 1978, she marched for the National Organization for Women in Washington, DC in hopes of passing the Equal Rights Amendment.

Mary currently lives in Glen Arbor, MI, with her dog, Rosalyn. Many of her children and grandchildren live nearby.